W9-CMC-844

TIME
FOR KIDS®
BEGINNING READER 1 *Science Scoops*

STORMS!

By the Editors of TIME FOR KIDS
WITH LESLIE DICKSTEIN

HarperCollins*Publishers*

About the Author: Leslie Dickstein has written about everything from travel and technology to health, nutrition, and parenting. She lives in New Jersey with her husband and two children.

To Mitch, my shelter from the storm, and to Harrison and Georgia, who fill every day with sunshine.

Special thanks to the National Weather Service office of public affairs for their time and expertise.   –L.D.

Library of Congress Cataloging-in-Publication Data is available.
ISBN 0-06-078204-8 (pbk.) — ISBN 0-06-078205-6 (trade)

1 2 3 4 5 6 7 8 9 10
First Edition

Copyright © by Time Inc.
TIME For Kids and the Red Border Design are Trademarks of Time Inc. used under license.

Photography and Illustration Credits:
Cover: Warren Faidley—Weatherstock; cover insert: Don Lloyd—Weatherstock; cover flap: Warren Faidley—Weatherstock; title pg: Warren Faidley—Weatherstock; pg. 3: Richard Hamilton Smith—Corbis; pp. 4–5: Osamu Honda—AP; pg. 4 (inset): John Courtney; pp. 6–7: Gary Meszaros—Bruce Coleman; pp. 8–9: Rob Matheson—Corbis; pg. 9 (inset): John Courtney; pp. 10–11: Adam Jones—Visuals Unlimited; pp. 12–13: Photodisc; pp. 14–15: Don Lloyd—Weatherstock; pp. 16–17: Alan R. Moller—Getty Images; pp. 18–19: Henry Romero—Reuters/Corbis; pp. 20–21: NOAA; pp. 22–23: J. Albert Diaz—The Miami Herald/SIPA; pp. 24–25: Richard Hutchings—Corbis; pp. 26–27: David Duprey—AP; pp. 28–29: Rick Gebhard—Marinette Eagle Herald/AP; pp. 30–31: Gary Yeowell—Getty Images; pg. 32 (blizzard): Richard Hutchings—AP; pg. 32 (flood): Osamu Honda—AP; pg. 32 (hail): Gary Meszaros—Bruce Coleman; pg. 32 (hurricane): NOAA; pg. 32 (lightning): Bob Matheson—Corbis; pg. 32 (tornado): Don Lloyd—Weatherstock.

Acknowledgments:
For TIME For Kids: Editorial Director: Keith Garton; Editor: Nelida Gonzalez Cutler; Art Director: Rachel Smith; Designer: Colleen Pidel; Photography Editor: Jill Tatara

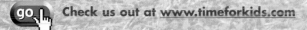

Check us out at www.timeforkids.com

Look up!
The clouds are big and dark.
A storm is coming.

Down comes the rain!
It is a thunderstorm.
There is lightning and thunder.
Heavy rains can cause flooding.

That Is Amazing!

There are about
sixteen million
thunderstorms
in the world
every year.

Sometimes rain freezes as it falls.
It turns to ice.
These pieces of ice are called hail.

Flash! Lightning streaks
across the sky.
It lights up the night.
Lightning is a giant spark
of electricity.

That Is Amazing!

The temperature near lightning is about 50,000° F. That is even hotter than the sun!

Boom! Thunder makes a loud sound.
It is caused by lightning.
Lightning heats the air around it.
Thunder is the sound of the air
being heated very quickly.

Lightning and thunder
happen at the same time.
You see lightning first.
That is because light
travels faster than sound.

Big thunderstorms can make a tornado.
This funnel-shaped cloud spins like a top.

Tornado winds blow very fast!
They act like a giant vacuum cleaner.
A tornado can lift objects.
It can even pull the roof off a house!

Here comes a hurricane!
Hurricanes are giant rainstorms
with strong winds.

The center of a hurricane
is called the eye.
It is calm in the eye.
It is not windy.
There are few clouds.

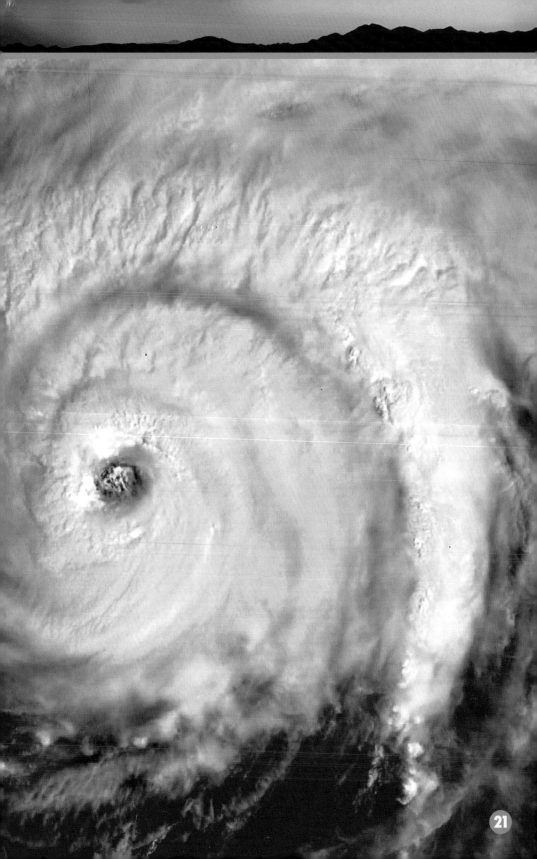

In the United States, hurricane season begins on June 1.
It ends on November 30.
In other parts of the world, hurricanes can happen at any time.

It is snowing!
If it snows for hours, it may
become a blizzard.
A blizzard is a huge snowstorm.

Strong winds blow the snow
into big drifts.
The snow is heavy.
It can break branches.

Brrrr! It is cold, cloudy, and rainy.
The rain turns to ice on cold surfaces.
This is an ice storm.

The sun is shining.
There is a rainbow.
The storm is over.

WORDS to Know

Blizzard: a snowstorm with strong winds

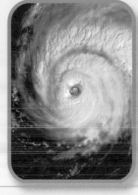

Hurricane: a huge windstorm and rainstorm

Flood: water covering land that is usually dry

Lightning: the flashing of light that is produced by a giant spark of electricity

Hail: pieces of ice that fall from storm clouds

Tornado: a funnel-shaped cloud that spins very fast